5 - STRING BASS METHOD

BY BRIAN EMMEL
LOW B TUNING

Cover Photo:
Thanks to Terry Dennis
for the use of the FERNANDES 5 string bass, Model APB - 100

ISBN 978-1-5742-4114-3
SAB 683-8022

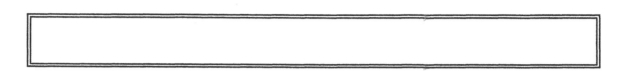

Special Thanks

I would like to thank the Musician's Institute of Hollywood California, John Waltrips Music Centers, Frank Green, Gards Music House, Peavey instruments, GHS strings, Ramona Emmel, Lisa Peters, David Celentano, and God who brought all these people together to help me obtain and complete this book.

This book is dedicated to Geddy Lee of Rush, whom over the years has given me inspiration and desire to progress in the field of music.

~Contents~

The Author

Brian Lee Emmel grew up in Northern Ohio where he began playing electric guitar at the age of 14, and later switched to bass guitar at 17. After playing in local top 40 bands he decided to devote his time to songwriting and formed a three piece original act which cut a 45 single that received airplay in Indiana, Michigan, and Ohio.

He has relocated to Los Angeles and has completed an education at the Musician's Institute (B.I.T.) in Hollywood, graduating in the top class.

Tablature Explanation

The tablature used here is written on a staff of five lines. Each line stands for a string on the bass. The highest line represents the first string, the lowest represents the fifth string, and so on. Numbers on the lines represent frets-1 stands for the first fret, 2 for second fret, and so on (see example below). A zero on any line means that the corresponding string is to be played "open" (unfretted). Notes to be played simultaneously are aligned vertically.

SLIDE or SLUR-
Sliding to the 5th fret from the 3rd fret using the same finger.

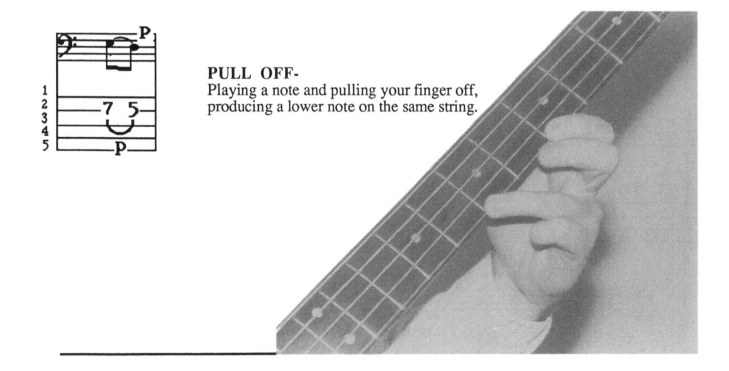

PULL OFF-
Playing a note and pulling your finger off, producing a lower note on the same string.

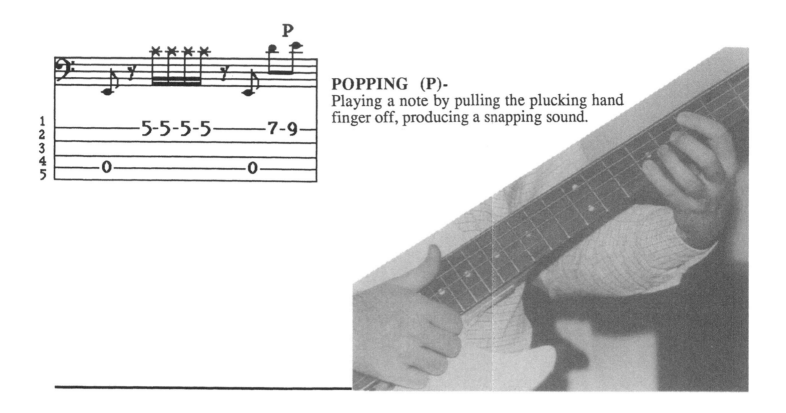

POPPING (P)-
Playing a note by pulling the plucking hand finger off, producing a snapping sound.

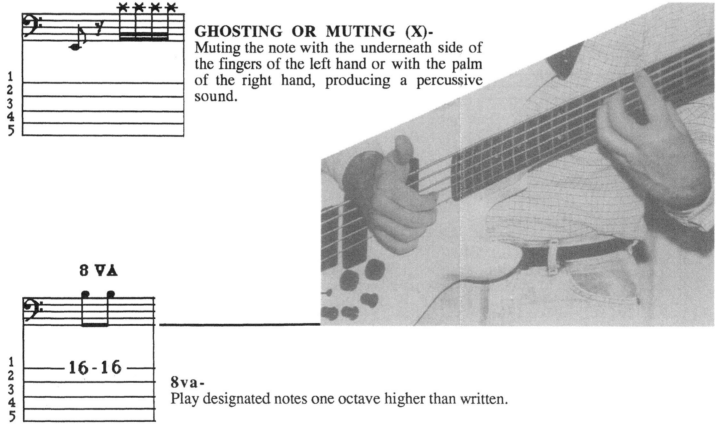

GHOSTING OR MUTING (X)-
Muting the note with the underneath side of the fingers of the left hand or with the palm of the right hand, producing a percussive sound.

8va-
Play designated notes one octave higher than written.

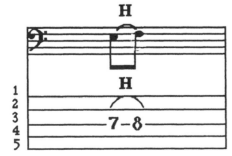

HAMMER ON-
Playing a note and striking a higher note on the same string with another finger, producing the higher note.

5 STRING VERSUS 4 STRING

Adapting to the 5 string is not as complicated as one may think. However, there are a few adjustments one must overcome such as neck width; the standard 4 string bass which we are accustomed to has a neck width of approximately 1 1/4" at the nut and 2 5/16" at the final fret. These measurements vary depending on the manufacturer.

The standard string gauges on the 4 string generally range from:
.040   .060   .075   .095 (G to E) in a light gauge set to
.055   .075   .090   .110 in the heavier gauge sets.

The 5 string neck width is a little wider, usually measuring 1 5/8" at the nut and 2 3/8" at the final fret, again, these will vary among the different manufacturers.

The 5 string gauges are the same as the standard from the G to E string with an additional B string which ranges from a .128 in a light gauge set to a .145 in a heavy.

I find the **GHS Progressives** to be very responsive to the touch, and produce the overall best tones in regular and five strings sets.

The string gauges I found to be most comfortable for the low B tuning are:

stb40-1st G, stb58-2nd D, stb78-3rd A, stb98-4th E, and stb121-5th B.

The above string guages are my personalized custom made set. The good people of GHS will proudly send your local dealer the same set upon special order.

MUSICAL STYLE

There is no limit as to what style of music can or should be played on the 5 string. Most 5 string applications are used in the contemporary pop format, because the low B is complimentary to the synthesized drums which together produce the emphasis of groove. **The 5 string bass is rapidly growing into the future.**

TUNINGS

The standard tuning on the 5 string bass is:

B -5th string
E -4th string
A -3rd string
D -2nd string
G -1st string

We call this "**Open Tuning**" because the harmonic interval from the low string to the high string is tuned in 4ths. The instrument is tuned in 4th intervals because in the natural major scale there are 8 steps that make up 1 octave from the root note to the next octave.

When tuned to "Open Tuning" there is access to a very sub low frequency which simulates the sounds of a bass synth. A lot of popular music utilizes synth bass because it's ultra low response generates a feeling of movement.

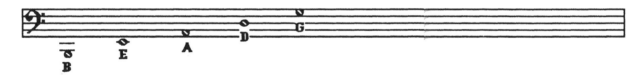

From each space to each line is one interval.
As you can see, there are 4th intervals between each open string.

Another tuning on the 5 string would be:

E-5th string;
A-4th string;
D-3rd string;
G-2nd string;
C-1st string.

This tuning would require replacing the string set with a regular 4 string gauge set, (see page 7) and replacing an even lighter gauge 1st string now tuned to a C. The C string gauge could range from a .26 to as high as a .22. This may require some experimenting. This set up is advantageous in chording notes and soloing, giving the bass more of a guitaresque tone, and the player a more polyphonic role.

This tuning is not as popular as the low B tuning for the mere fact that a bassist's role is to support or be the lower frequency foundation in music. In this book some examples will be given for the high C tuning but our primary focus will be on the low B application.

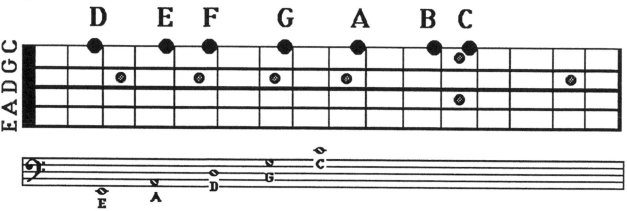

HOW TO PRACTICE
(Notes on the Neck)

Now that we've added a new dimension to our bass playing we should become familiar not only with an additional string, but with the whole instrument in general. The objective to this exercise is to get familiar with "notes on the neck". First, set a metronome to a comfortable setting, example, quarter note=72, start with all the B notes from low to high then reverse it from high to low.

With each pulse of the metronome, we should be able to play, consecutively, every B on the neck. I've also included some other note finding examples. As you progress with all 12 notes of the chromatic scale increase the metronome tempo just to make it exciting.

EX . 1

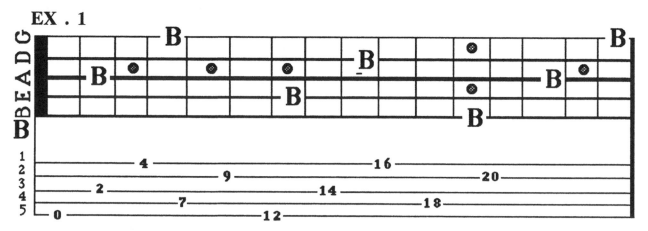

E

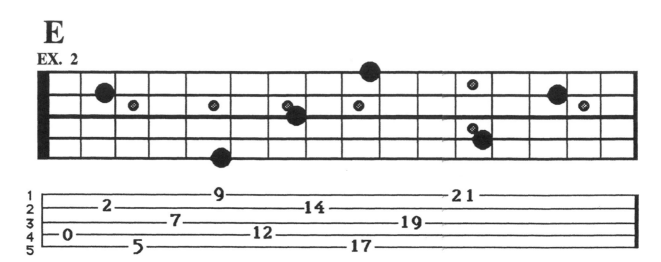

B flat

EX. 3

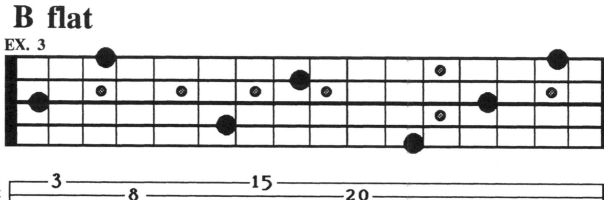

E flat

EX. 4

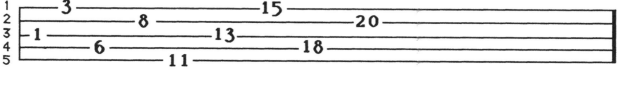

The Major or Ionian Scale

Now the fun begins. We are going to get acquainted with the 5 string bass by first, learning the major scale on the low B string, just to get familiar with the feel of a heavier string and slightly wider neck.

The numbers in parenthesis below the dot represent proper fingering. By using this formula you will notice a faster technique to get up and down the neck using fewer hand movements.

EX . 1
C major

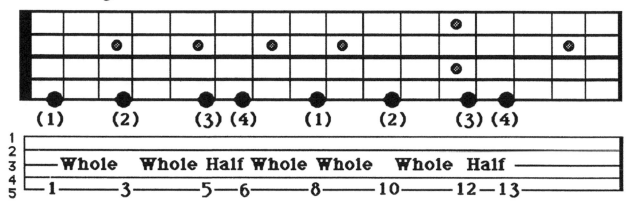

Notice the step formula for the major scale:
WHOLE   WHOLE   HALF   WHOLE   WHOLE   WHOLE   HALF

EX. 2
G major
(The step formula remaines the same)

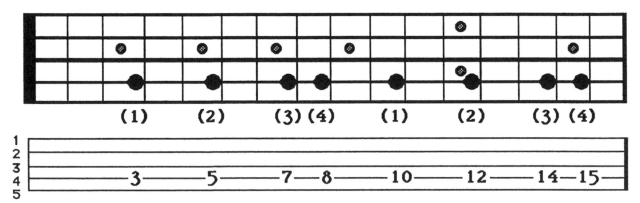

11

Now we will learn the major scale over the entire fret board, starting on the low B string and incorporating the adjacent 4 strings.

EX . 1

C major

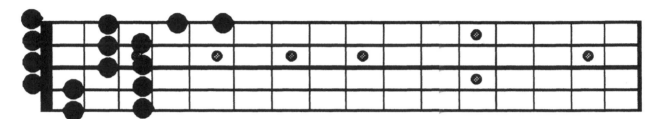

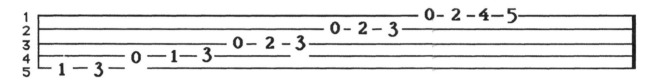

EX. 2

G major

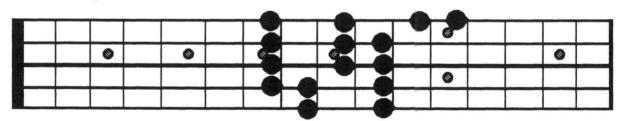

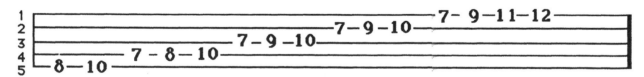

Scale within a 5 fret area

Next, we will learn the same major scale within a 5 fret area of the neck, starting on the low B and going through all 12 keys. This exercise should be applied in all 12 keys from it's root position starting on the B string. Then move the exercise up one fret at a time.

This exercise will show us how to make better use of all the notes in any given key by using virtually no hand shifting. **Note: On the cassette tape this is played as one continous exercise.**

EX . 1

C major

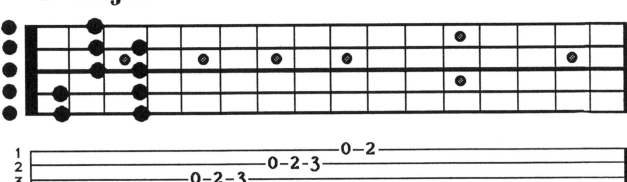

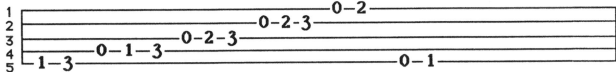

Play through all these keys in one attempt, each example should flow into each other.

Db major

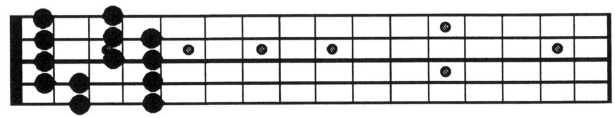

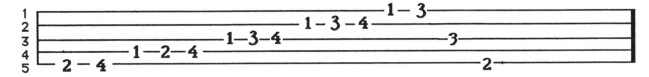

D major

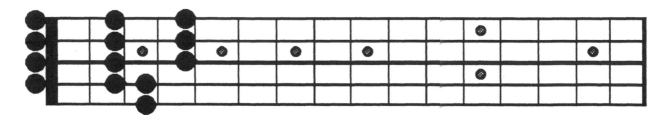

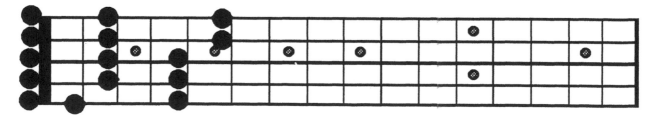

Now we will start the E major scale on the E string and after we play the note A we have access to the low B string to complete the scale an octave lower. Then proceed playing the scale over the remaining four fret string area.

Eb major

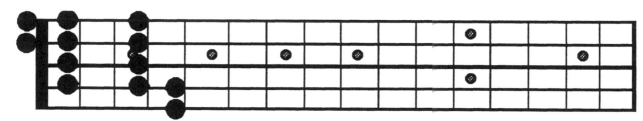

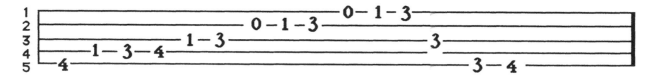

E major

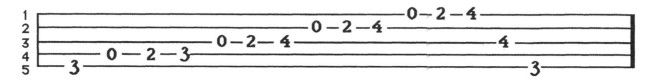

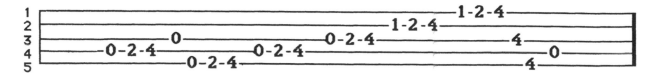

F major

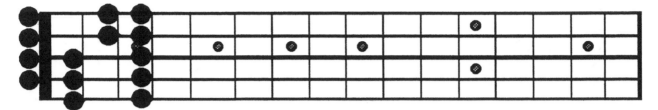

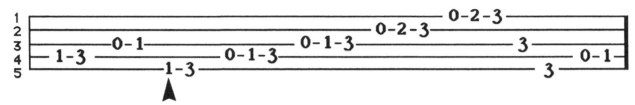

We can also start the scale on the C note of the low B string.

Gb major

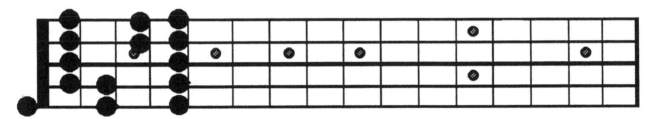

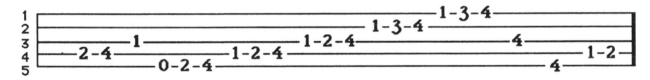

G major

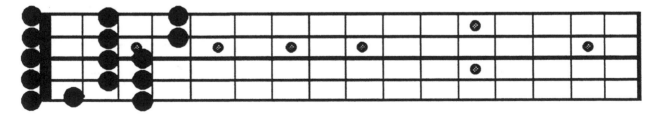

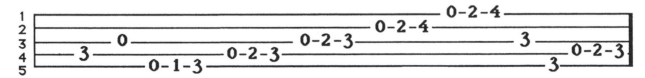

A flat major

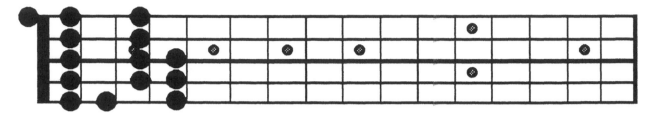

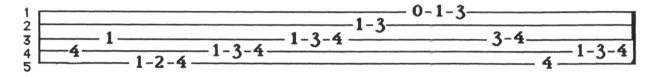

A major

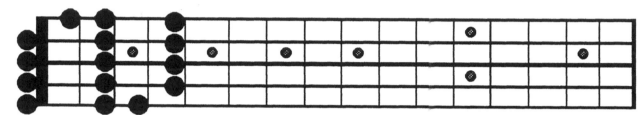

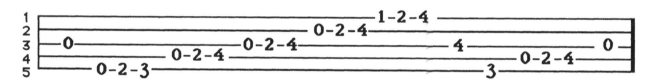

B major

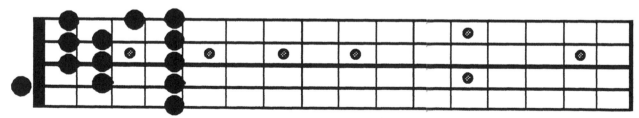

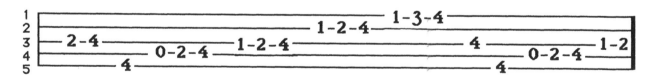

Remember this entire exercise is to get us more familiar with the low B string. Although we completed all 12 keys, think of this entire exercise as being in only one key. Now move it up one half step and repeat it in the new key of C# or Db.

NOTE: All these exercises should be executed with a metronome.
Increase the tempo with your progression.

Minor 2nd Interval

This example illustrates minor 2nd intervals.
As you can see these are the shortest intervals, or distance between chord tones.

EX. 1

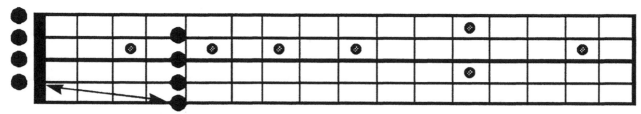

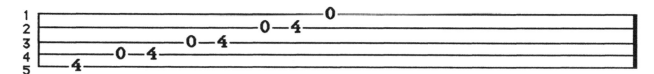

Here's another example of a minor 2nd interval. Also known as one-half step.
From all open strings to the 1st fret of that same string is a minor 2nd interval.

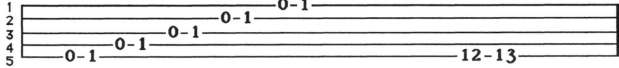

Major 2nd Interval

From the 3rd fret to the preceding open string is the distance of a major 2nd interval.
From all open strings to the 2nd fret of that same string is a major 2nd interval.

EX. 2

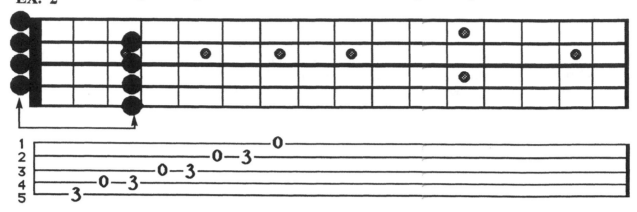

Here's another example of a major 2nd interval. Also known as one-whole step.

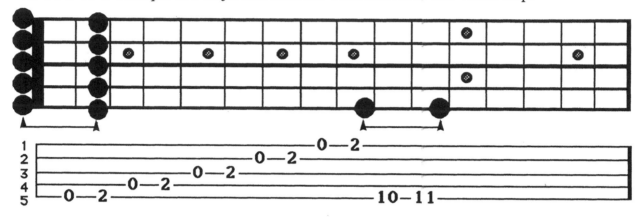

Minor 3rd Interval

EX. 3   From all open strings to the 1st fret of same string is a minor 3rd interval.

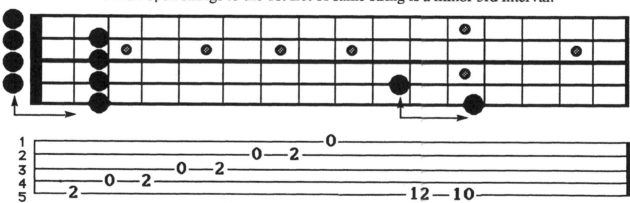

Here's another example of a minor 3rd interval.

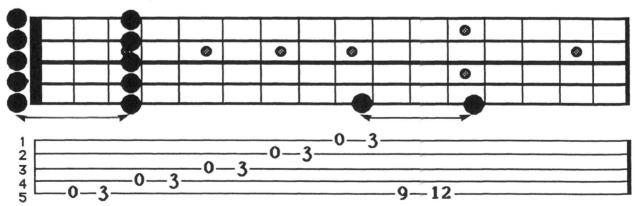

Major 3rd Intervals

EX. 4

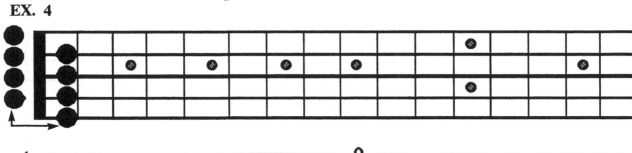

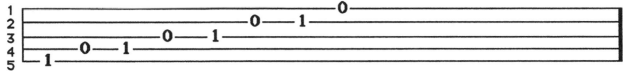

This example illustrates how the major 3rd interval is equal to two whole steps.

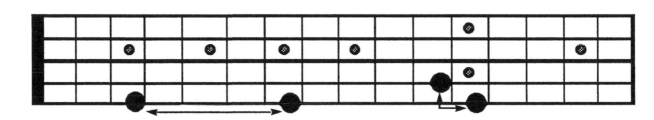

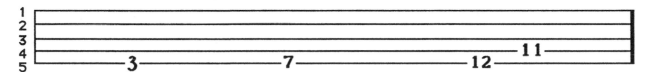

Perfect 4ths.

EX. 5

Perfect 4ths are easy to recognize because they are placed beside each other in parallel.

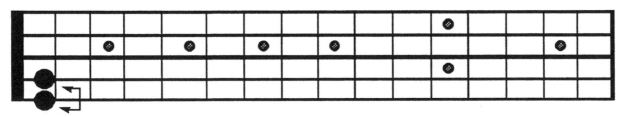

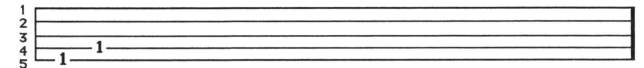

Perfect 5ths.

These examples illustrate perfect 5th interval shapes.
This is a common tone heard in major and minor harmonies.

EX. 6

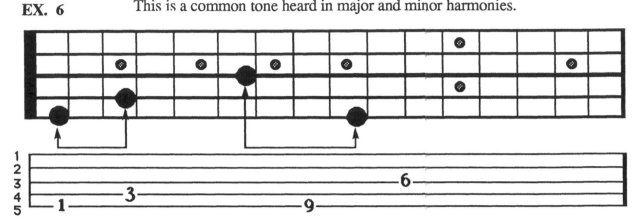

Note: Remember these are only examples
You should experiment with these shapes over the entire fretboard.

Minor 6th Intervals

EX. 7

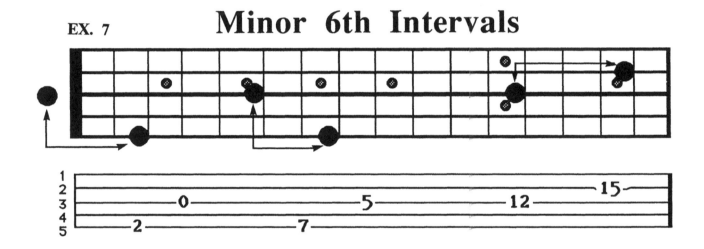

Major 6th Intervals

EX. 8

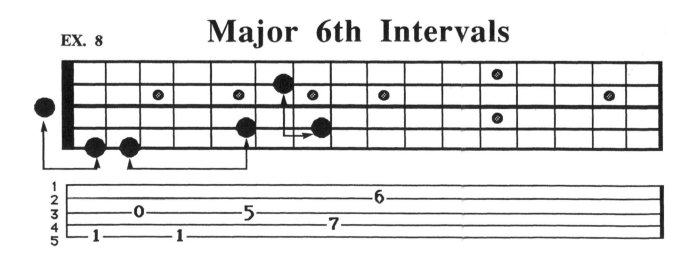

Minor 7th Intervals

This minor 7th shape is similar to the perfect 4th interval shape, except it skips one string over.

EX. 9

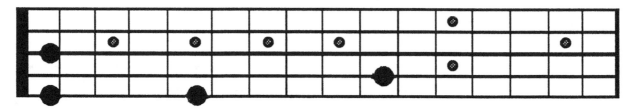

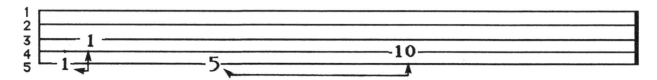

Major 7th Intervals

And finally the major 7th interval, also known as the leading tone, because if we we're to extend the 7th tone for one half step, we would resolve on the root notes octave.

EX. 10

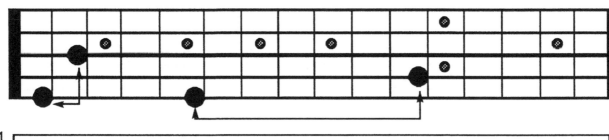

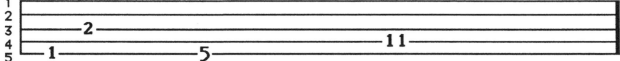

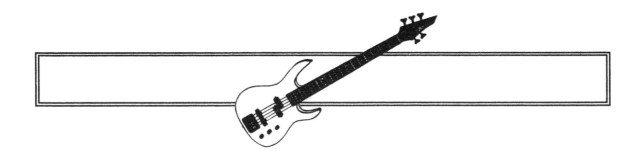

The major scale in the key of C

Set the metronome to quarter note =72 and play the interval patterns illustrated going forward and reverse. Practice the interval in C then move up one step and keep moving up until all 12 keys are played and increase the metronome speed as you progress. Your ear will soon be able to naturally pick out these harmonic relationships on whatever music media you listen to.

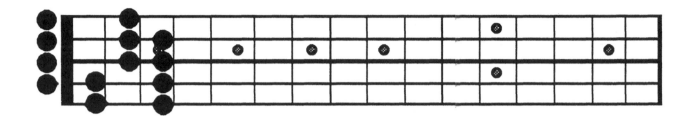

Notice by looking at the diagram, how this pattern is composed of major and minor 2nd intervals.

EX. 1

Major and Minor 3rd Intervals

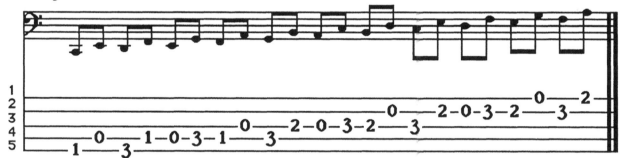

22

Tri-Tone Interval

Notice: The augmented interval (F to B) on the E & A strings. This interval is called a "Tri-Tone". This interval exists on all 4th & 5th intervals because it's the leading tone into the octave.

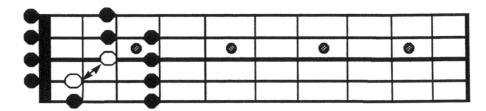

The 4th and 5th intervals are called perfect intervals, because they remain unchanged in both, the major and minor scales.

Perfect 4th Intervals

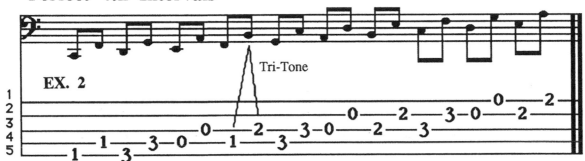

Perfect 5th Intervals

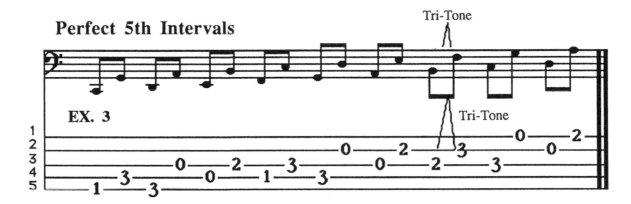

Major and Minor 6th Intervals

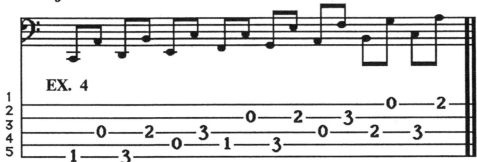

Major and Minor 7th Intervals

ARPEGGIOS

This chapter illustrates the notes which make up chords. Arpeggios are single notes played consecutively, these notes outline the chords which are played by guitarists, pianists, etc..

The following examples illustrates four different types of Arpeggios, each of which supplement the four types of chords which belong to the harmonized major family.
Major 7, Minor 7, Dominant 7, Half diminished or Minor flat 5.

Note:
On the cassette tape this is played as one continous exercise.

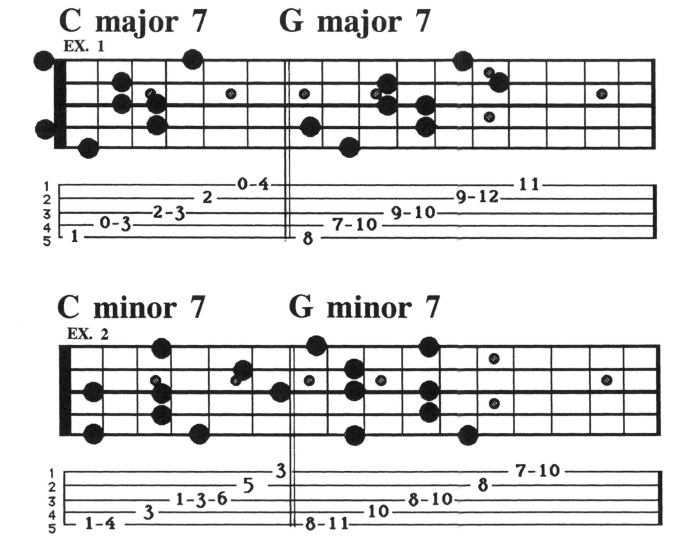

C dominant 7 G dominant 7

EX. 3

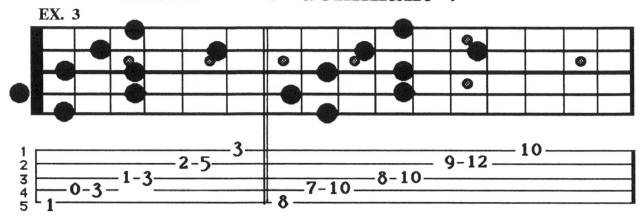

C half diminished G half diminished

EX. 4

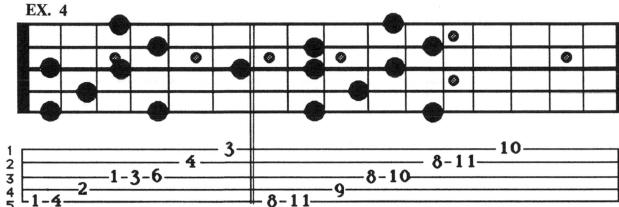

The next examples illustrate all **seven** Arpeggios from the harmonized major scale. Practice this exercise in all 12 keys. The chord structure in the harmonized major scale is: **major, minor, minor, major, major (Dominant 7), half diminished or minor.**

C major 7 (C maj 7)

EX. 1

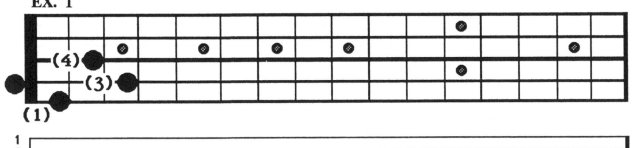

D minor 7 (Dmi7)

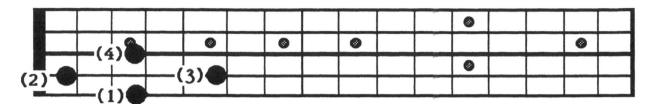

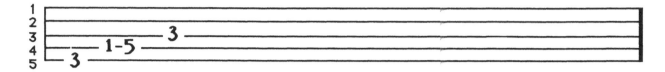

E minor 7 (E mi 7)

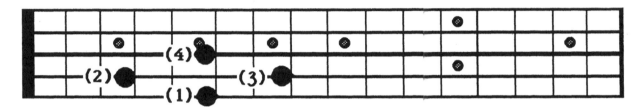

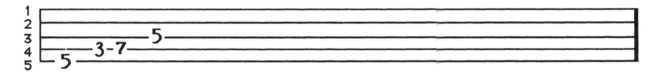

F major 7 (F maj7)

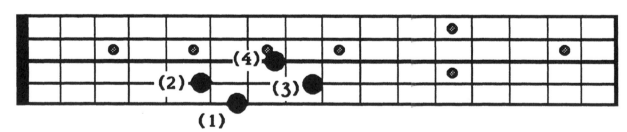

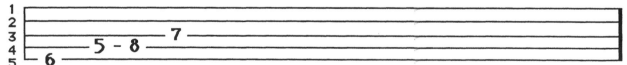

G Dominant 7 (G7)

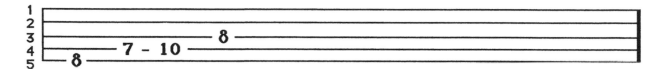

A minor 7 (A mi7)

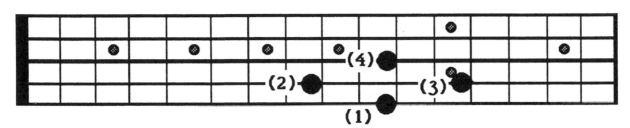

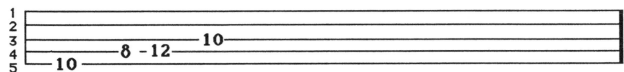

B minor 7 flat 5 (B mi7-5)

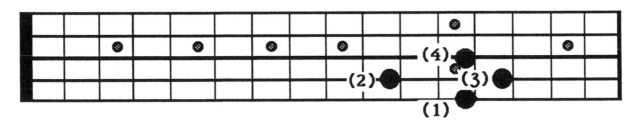

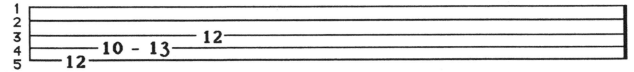

C major 7

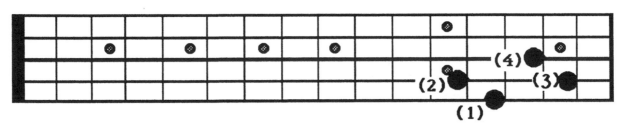

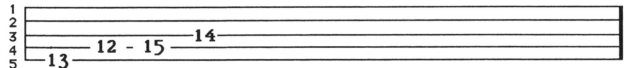

These examples will illustrate different arpeggiated voicings. (The natural construction of a maj7 chord is numbered (1,3,5,7), and in this exercise we scramble the natural formula, using 1-5-7-3, 1-7-5-3, 5-1-3-7, 5-7-1-3, 7-3-5-1, 3-7-5-1, and 3-1-7-5 underneath the actual chords they belong to. Play this with a friend who plays guitar or piano, or if you can, play these chord progressions into a tape recorder and playing it back, play the arpeggios.

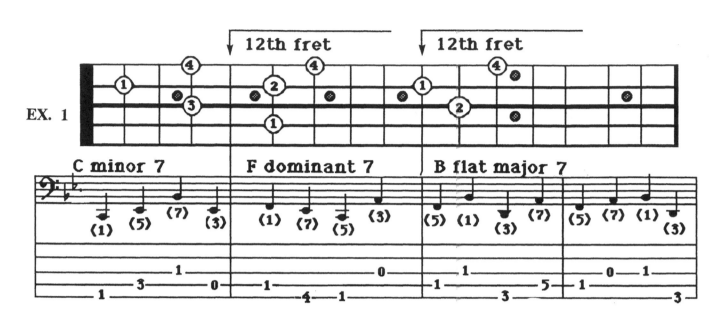

EX. 1

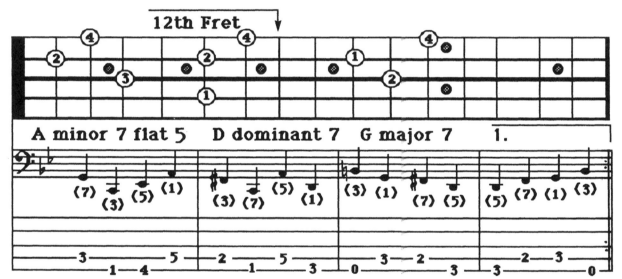

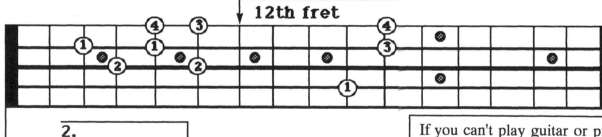

If you can't play guitar or piano, and you don't have any friends that could do this for you, these examples shows the fretboard diagram of the chord voicings on the bass. This is a neat trick all bass players should pick up on, because if you are ever confronted with a chord chart and not familiar with the song, you could define the melody for yourself, without having someone else play it for you.

28

CHORDS

Chords are not a primary function of the bass, but can be used to ornament certain musical areas given at the right time and in the right place. This chapter will illustrate how to make chords on the bass and how to apply them over a chord chart so we can hear what type of tonalities and melodies are in a given tune.

C major 7

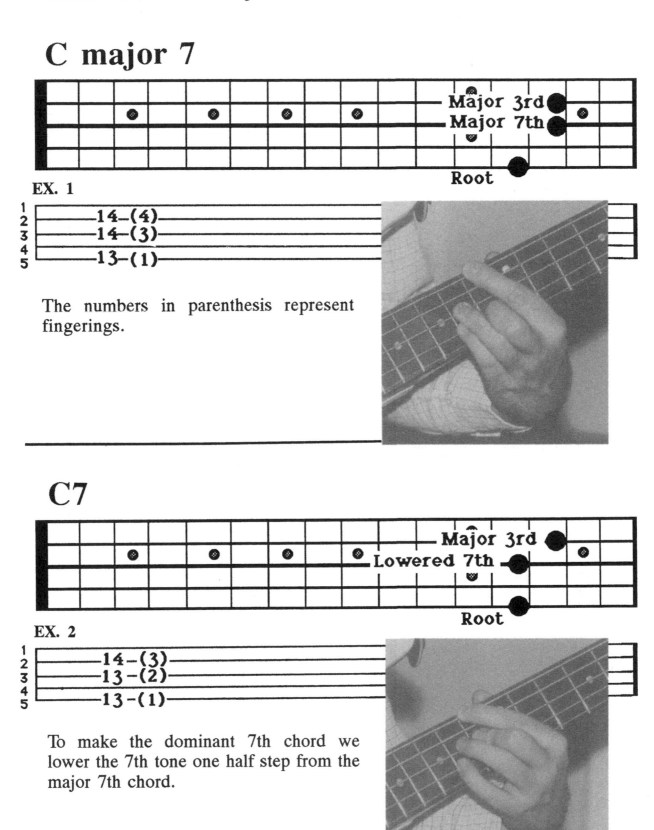

EX. 1

The numbers in parenthesis represent fingerings.

C7

EX. 2

To make the dominant 7th chord we lower the 7th tone one half step from the major 7th chord.

C mi 7

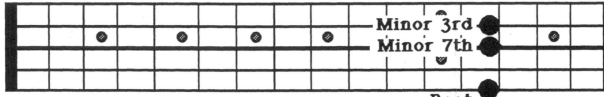

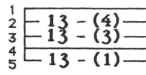

EX. 3

```
1 ┌─ 13 - (4) ──────────
2 │   13 - (4)
3 │   13 - (3) ──────────
4 │   13 - (1) ──────────
5 └─ 13 - (1) ──────────
```

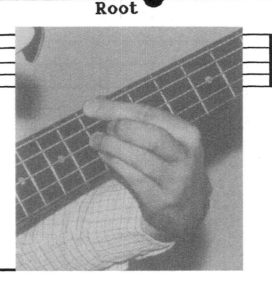

Now we lower the major 3rd and we have a minor 7th chord.

C mi 7-5

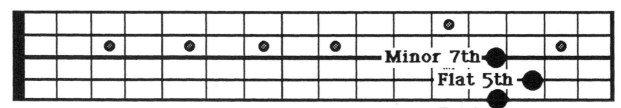

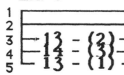

EX. 4

```
1 ──────────────────────
2 ──────────────────────
3  →  13 = (2) ──────────
4     14 = (3) ──────────
5     13 = (1) ──────────
```

This is a common jazz chord, note that the previous chords contained no 5th interval because the 3rd and 7th tones expressed the tonality of the given chord. The flat 5th interval must be played in this chord to express it's tonality.

Move these chord forms over the entire fretboard, using the root note as your index to establish the new chord name.

C 6

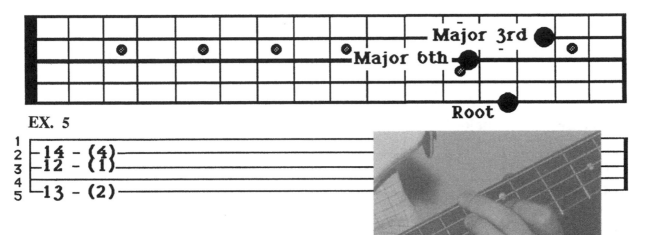

EX. 5

```
1 ┌─ 14 ─ {4} ───────
2 │
3 ├─ 12 ─ {1} ───────
4 │
5 └─ 13 ─ (2) ───────
```

C mi6

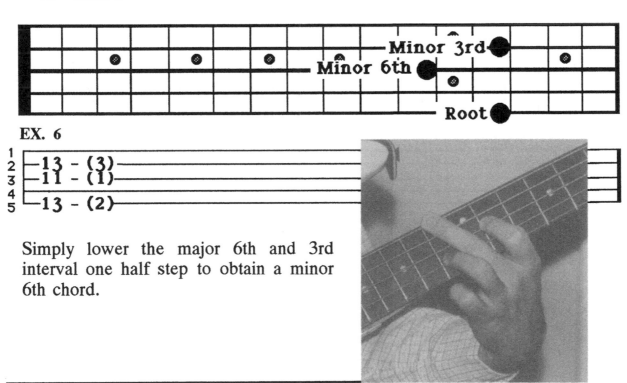

EX. 6

```
1 ┌─ 13 ─ (3) ───────
2 │
3 ├─ 11 ─ (1) ───────
4 │
5 └─ 13 ─ (2) ───────
```

Simply lower the major 6th and 3rd interval one half step to obtain a minor 6th chord.

C sus.

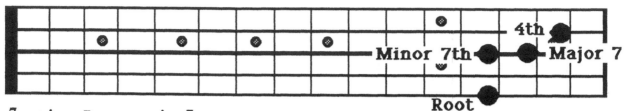

EX. 7   minor 7   major 7

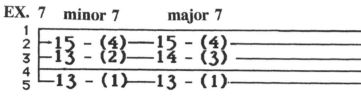

```
1
2 ─15 ─ (4)──15 ─ (4)──────
3 ─13 ─ (2)──14 ─ (3)──────
4
5 ─13 ─ (1)──13 ─ (1)──────
```

The suspended chord can be played with a major or dominant 7 tonality.

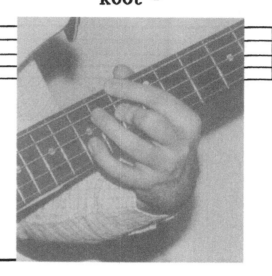

C dim.

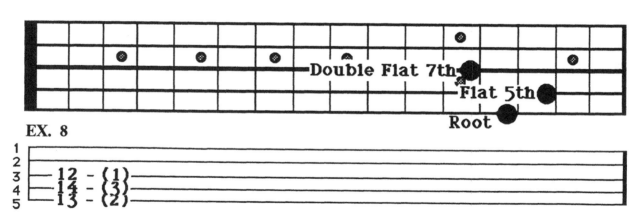

EX. 8

```
1
2
3 ─12 ─ (1)────────
4 ─14 ─ (3)────────
5 ─13 ─ (2)────────
```

A fully diminished chord contains the flat 5 and a double flat 7th interval. The double flat 7 is harmonically equivalent to major 6th interval.

The following examples will illustrate some chord inversions. In the first example we have a C major chord with the 3rd in the bass, or root position. This is known as 1st inversion.

C major-1st inversion

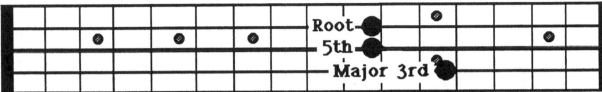

EX. 1

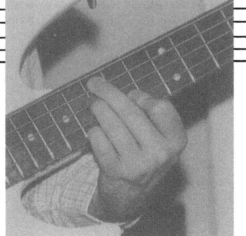

C major-2nd inversion

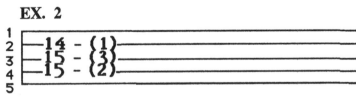

EX. 2

If we move the 5th of the chord to the root position, we are in 2nd inversion.

C major-3rd inversion

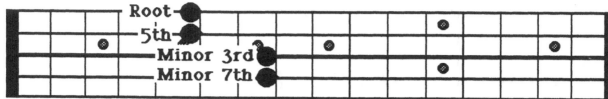

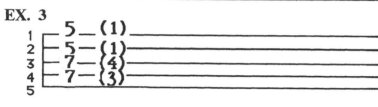

EX. 3

```
    5 — (1)
1 ┌ 5 — (1)
2 ├ 7 — (4)
3 ├ 7 — (3)
4 └
5
```

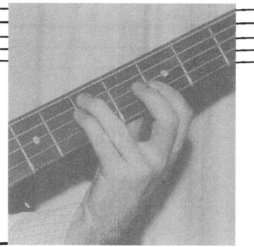

The last type of inversion is called 3rd inversion. It occurs when there is a 7 tone places in the root position.

C minor-1st inversion

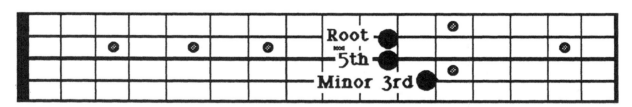

EX. 4

```
1 ┌
2 ├ 10 - (1)
3 ├ 10 - (1)
4 └ 11 - (2)
5
```

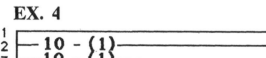

Resembles a major 6 chord.

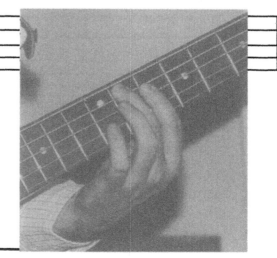

C minor-2nd inversion

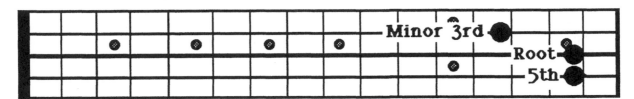

Minor 3rd
Root
5th

EX. 5

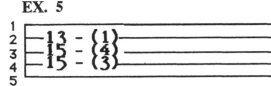

Chord inversions add a different dimension or harmony when played against certain chords, although as bass players, our function is primarily focused on the root notes.

C minor 7-3rd inversion

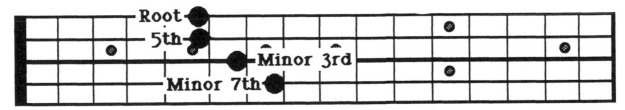

Root
5th
Minor 3rd
Minor 7th

EX. 6

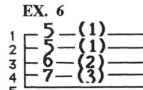

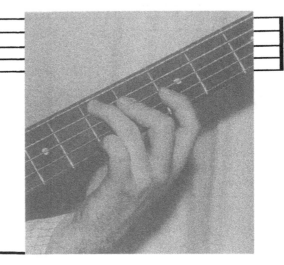

CHORD PROGRESSION

The 2.5.1, progressions get their numeral identity from the nature of their position in the harmonized major scale. If harmonized using 3 notes of the scale we get: 1 chord is major, 2 chord-minor, 3 chord- minor, 4 chord-major, 5 chord-major, 6 chord-minor, and the 7th chord-minor or diminished, if harmonized using 4 notes of the scale we get: the 1 chord is a major 7th, 2 chord-minor 7th, 3 chord-minor 7th, 4 chord-major 7th, 5 chord-dominant 7th, 6 chord-minor 7th, 7 chord- minor 7-flat 5 chord.

EX. 1

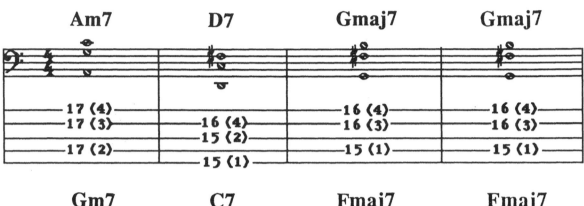

POP SYNTH BASS LINES

Today's contemporary songs contain synth bass instead of electric bass. This chapter will show you some synth bass licks. Notice how these parts created by most keyboardists differ from how we bass players think. This first example is not notated in this book. I left it this way for you to sharpen your ear training skills from what you 've learned so far, this blank page is left open for you to transcribe. **Hint: Key of Bb.**

EX . 1

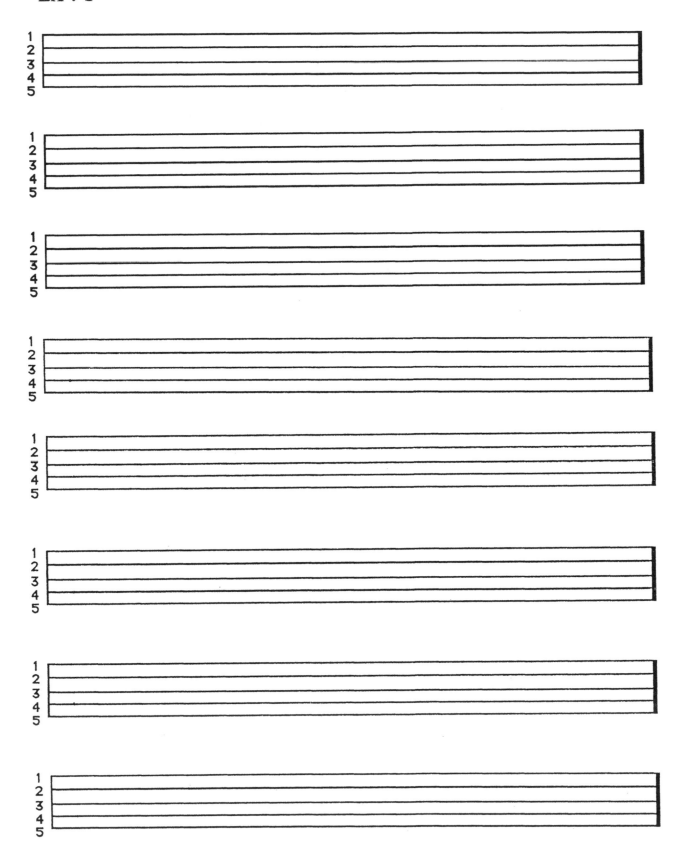

This example is in the style of Peter Gabriel, and is intended to be primarily a bass rhythm solo accompanied by drums and percussion only. Note the hammer's and pops.

Sinking Sun

EX. 2

By Brian Emmel

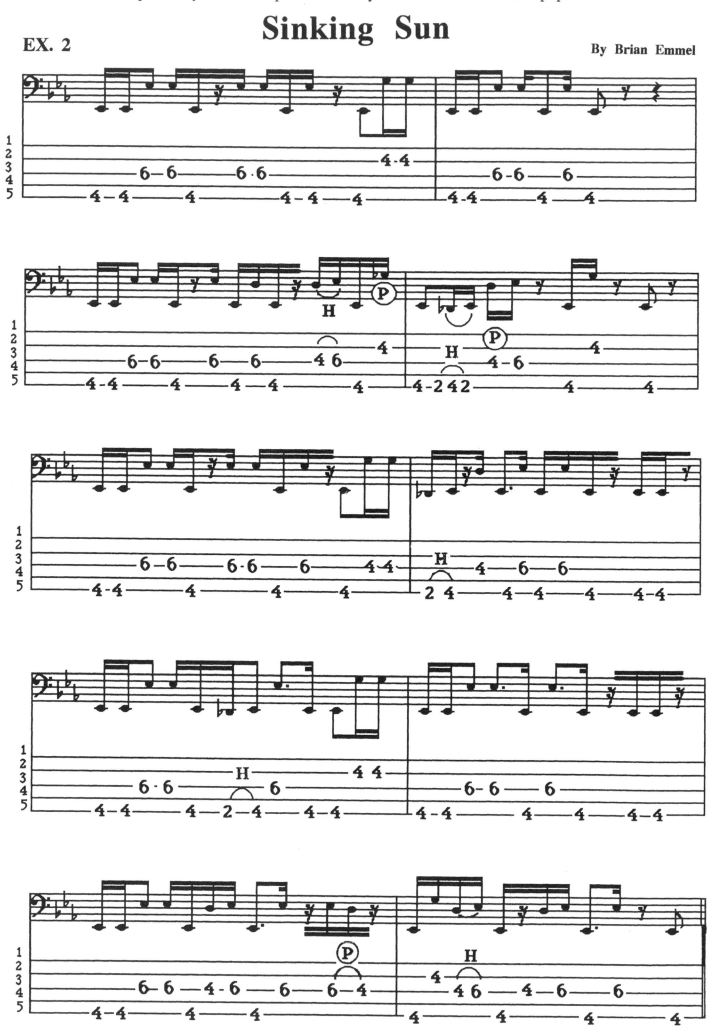

The style simulates "Mike and The Mechanics" which incorporates pumping single note synth bass lines. To get familiar with this style set a metronome at a comfortable tempo and practice this bass line by achieving smooth staccato driving eighth notes over the selected tempo using a pick or two finger technique. Sounds and looks easy but if you were to replace or play with this sequenced bass line in a studio, any default in timing or technique would be very disturbing.

WHEN TWO HEARTS COLLIDE

EX. 3

By Brian Emmel

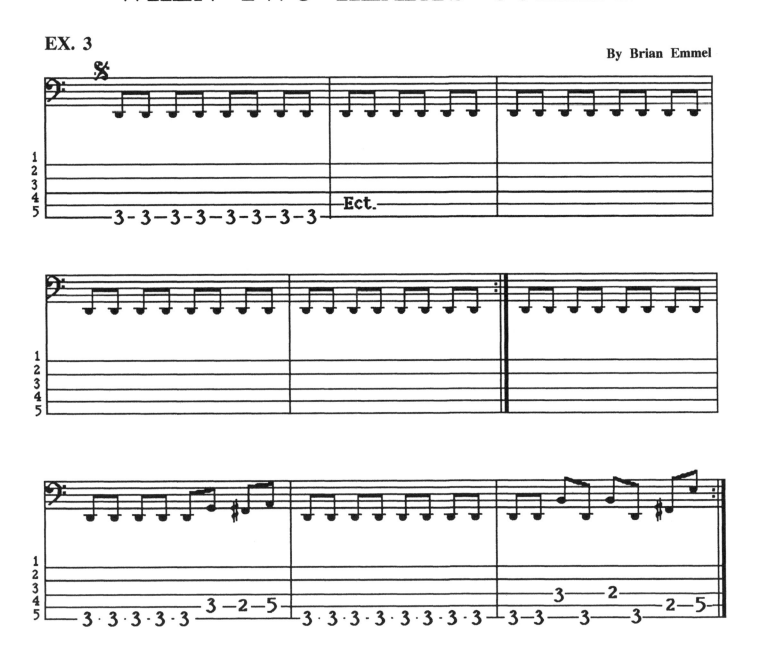

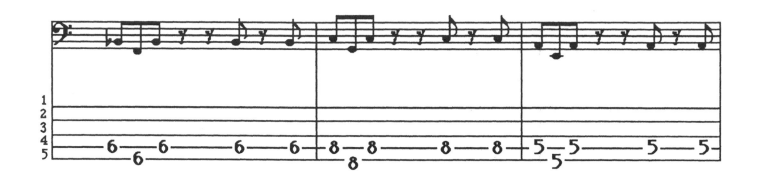

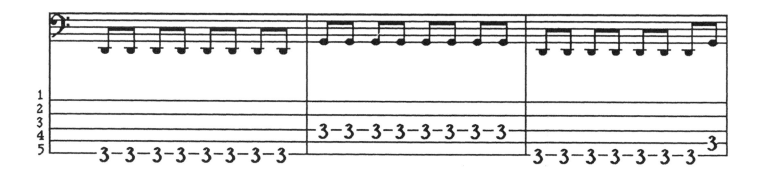

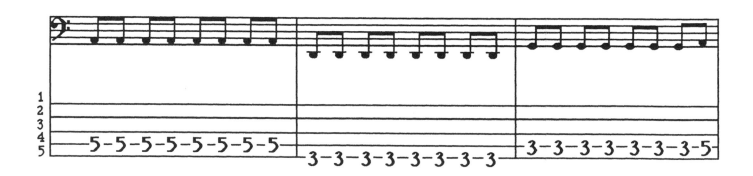

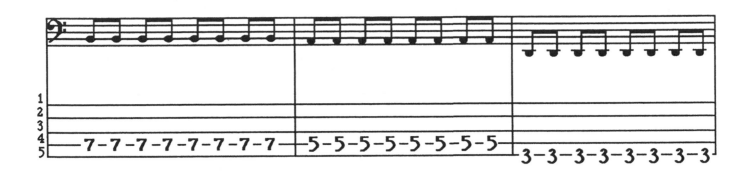

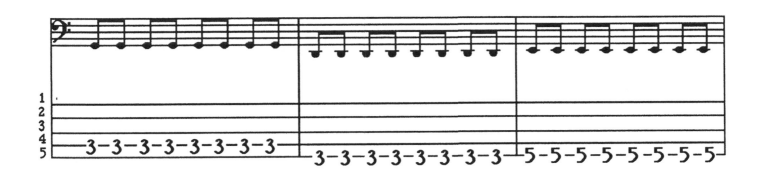

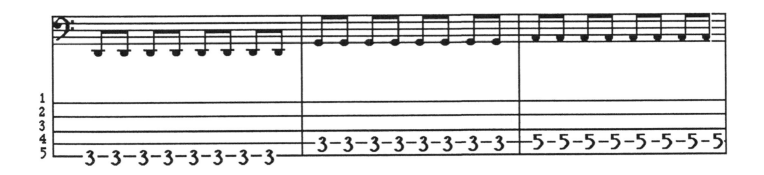

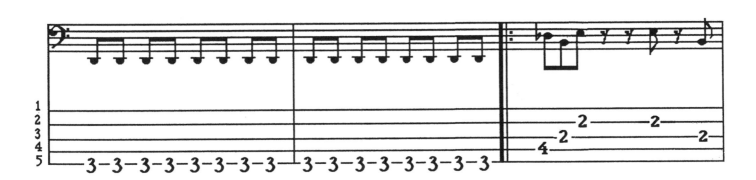

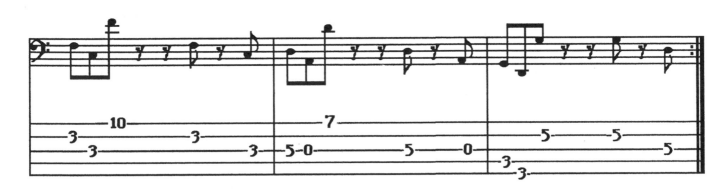

WALKING BASS LINES

In this chapter I will demonstrate how to approach 5 string Walking Bass Lines. The first example is a 12 bar jazz blues progression. Get a friend to play the chord progression's and walk the bass over the chords. Try to create your own walking line over this progression. The objective to playing or creating a good walking bass line is to have a smooth contour of note and tonal arrangement. Notes should be played close to each other without large intervallic leaps.

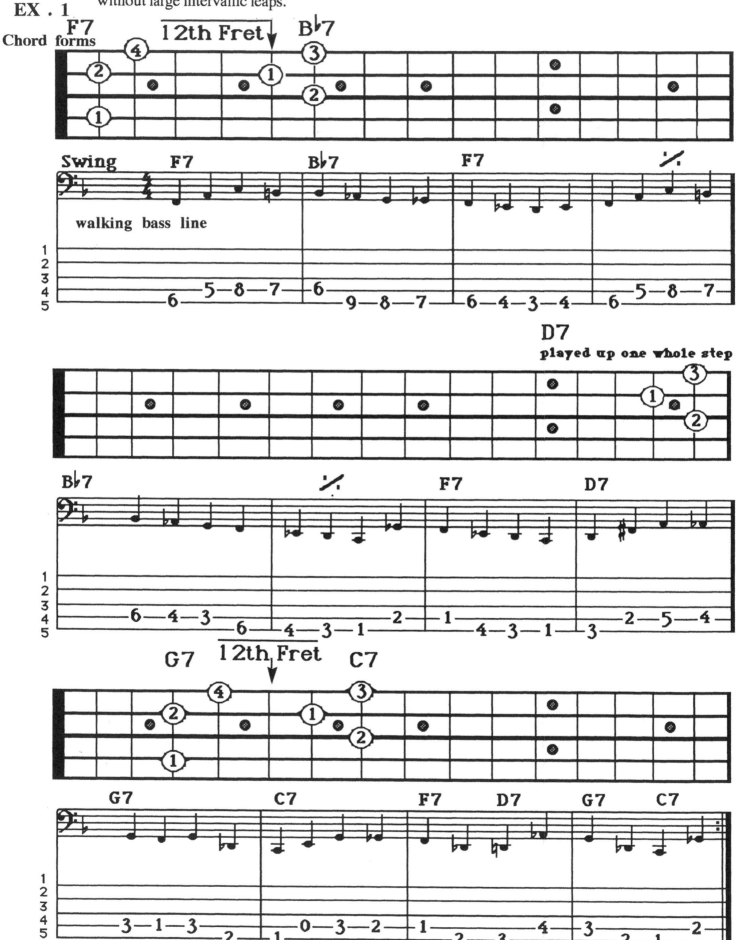

This second example is another popular chord progression used in jazz. The same rules apply as in the first example but this time play with a drum machine over a shuffle feel. In a shuffle feel the string beats are the 1st and 3rd notes of a 16th note grouping for example,

EX. 2

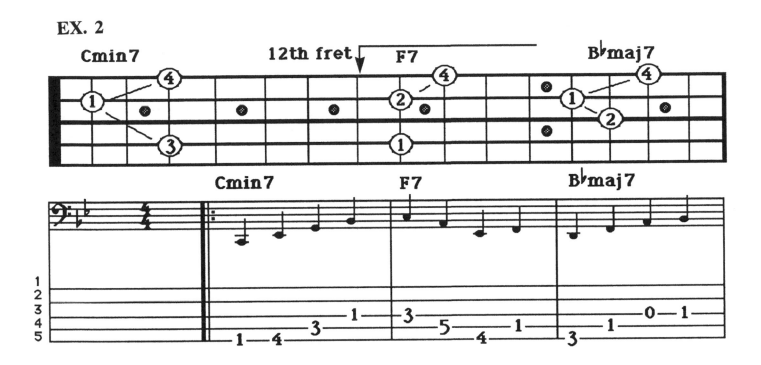

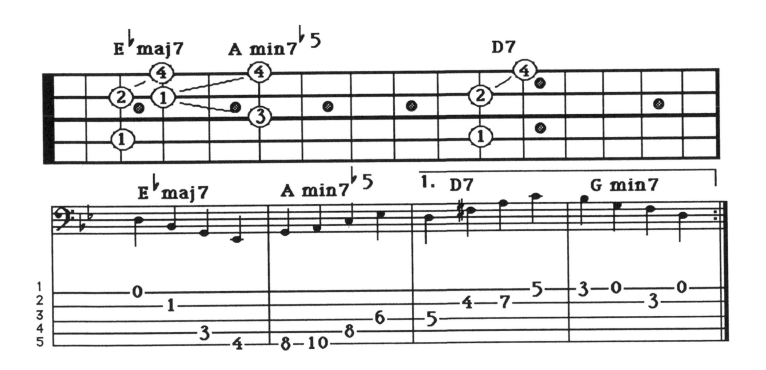

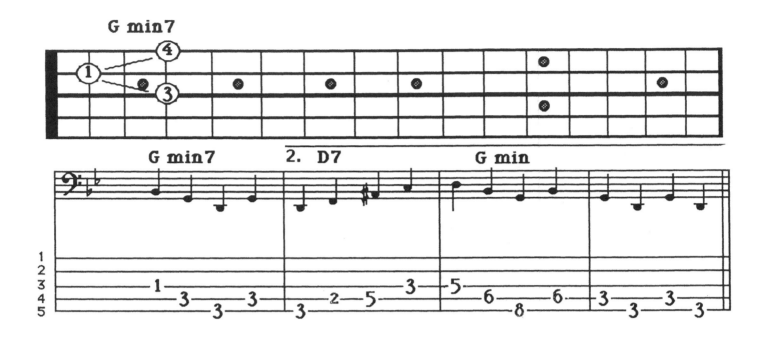

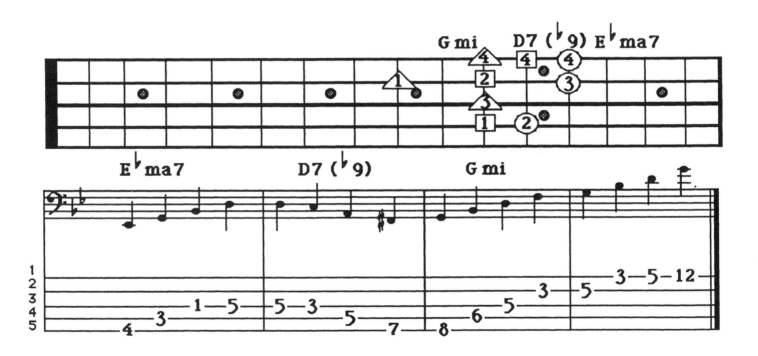

This exercise is different from the first two, in that although it too has a smooth connecting arrangement of notes, the notes are never more than one whole step away from a qualified chord tone. This creates an outside jazz sound and again requires minimal shifting or hand movement.

EX. 3

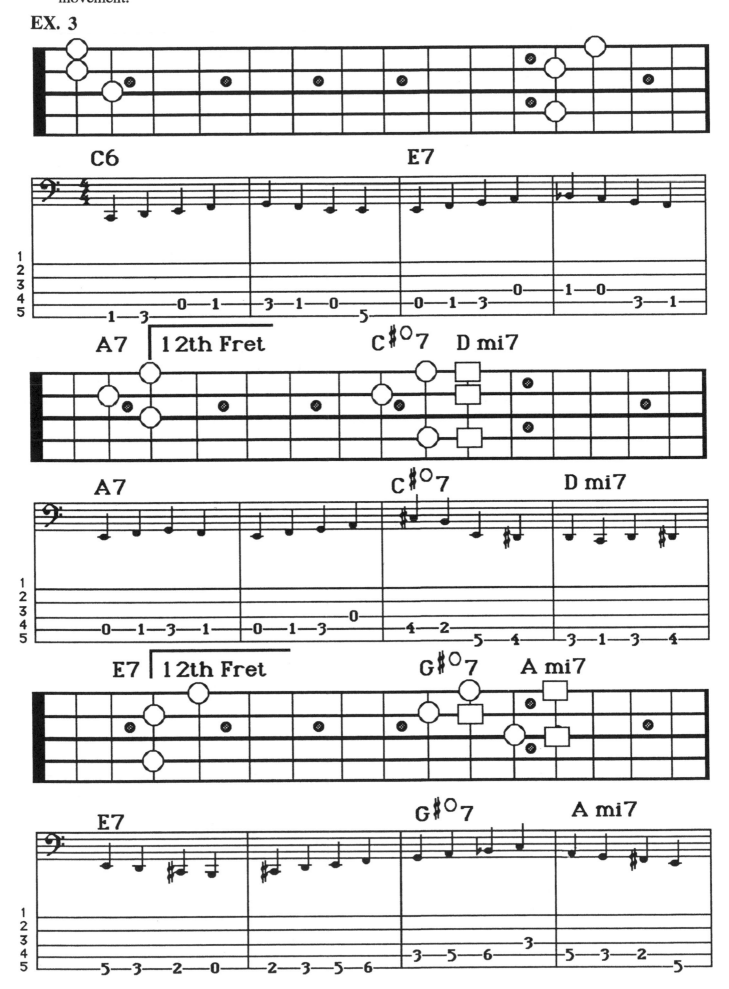

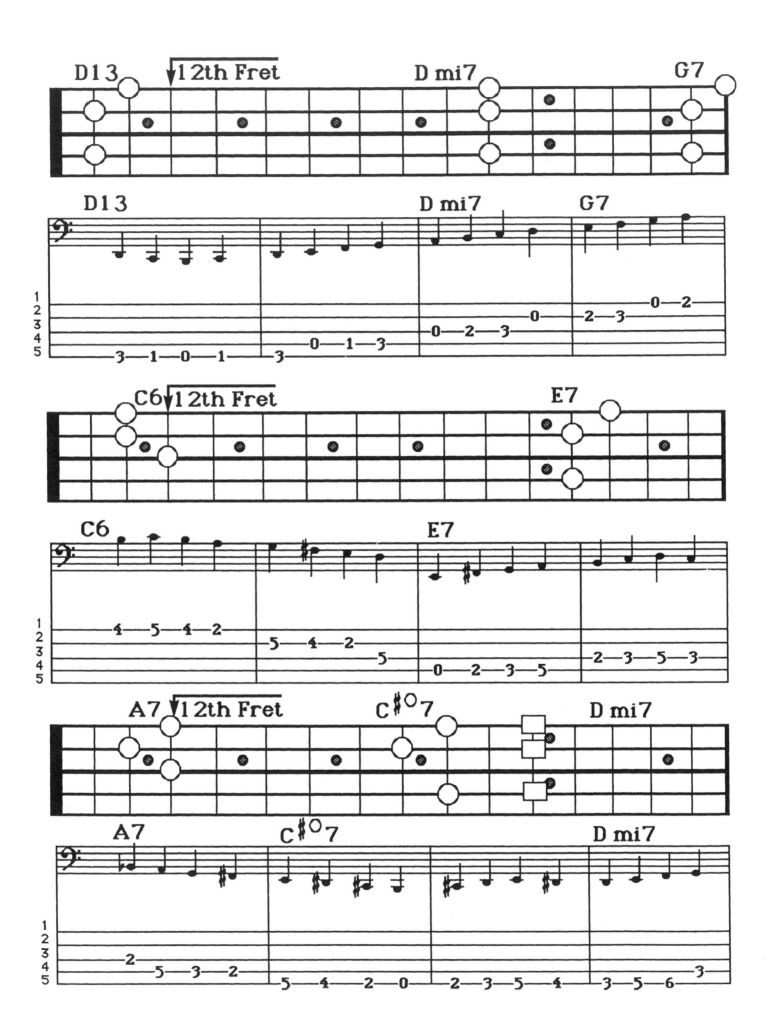

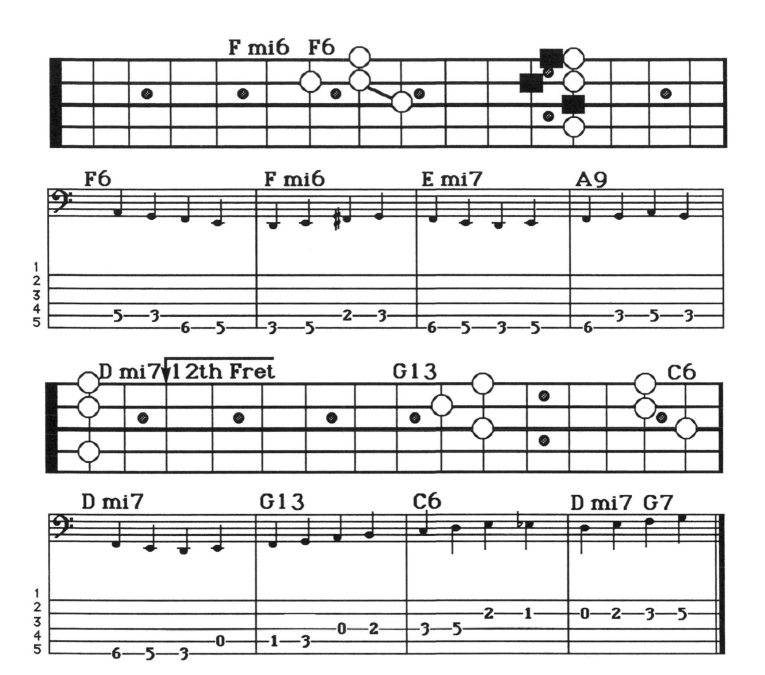

COUNTRY

This chapter will give you and idea of how to apply the low B string over some country tunes which I've written. The 5 string is excellent for country music because of the simplistic style for the bass, the low B string when combined with the drums, gives the music a bigger dynamic impression.

Company of Angels

EX . 1

By Brian Emmel

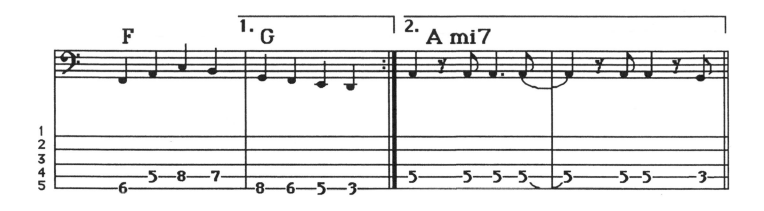

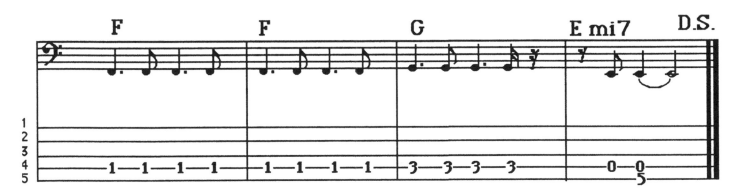

Hold Me and Tell Me

EX. 2

By Brian Emmel

CLASSICAL

This chapter will demonstrate how the 5 string can be applied to playing classical music. The 5th string can be real handy for this musical style because some notation for the bass cleff is written below the octave. Example 1 is an excerpt from Stravinsky's "Firebird Suite". This example is great for applying the low B string in a sight reading.

This song is not on the Cassette tape.

Firebird Suite

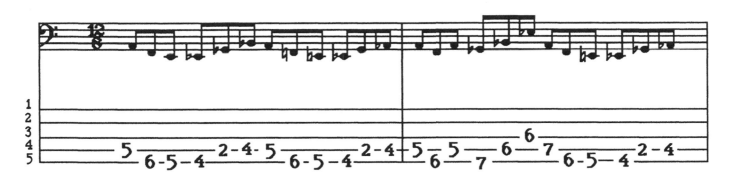

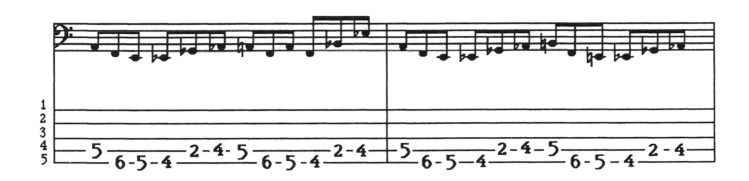

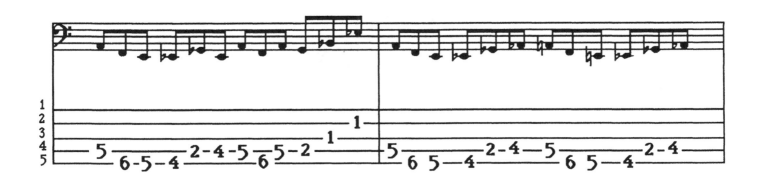

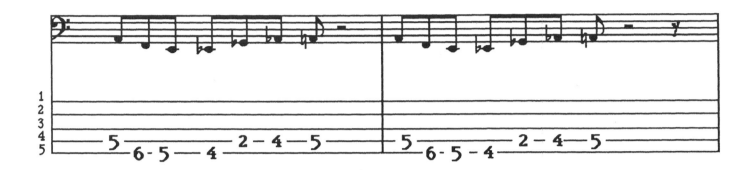

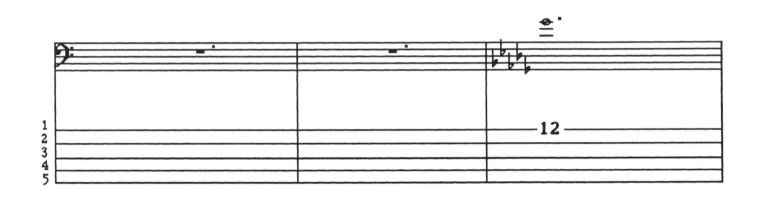

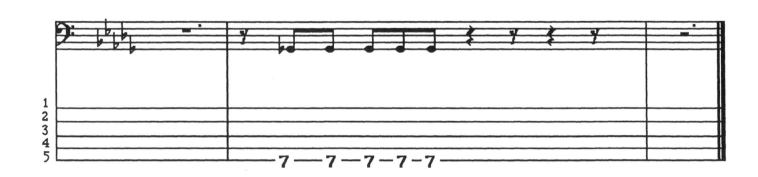

(E-A-D-G-C tuning)

This is the J. S. Bach's composition "Gavotte II". This exercise in intended for the E-A-D-G-C tuning because the range extends above the octave. Notice how this tuning relieves a lot excessive hand movement.

This song is not on the Cassette tape.

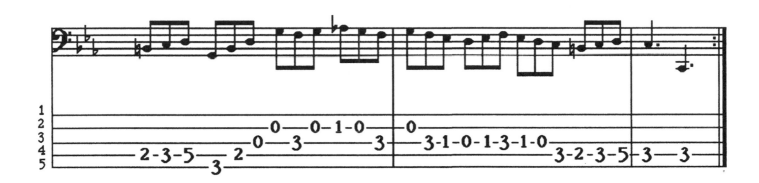

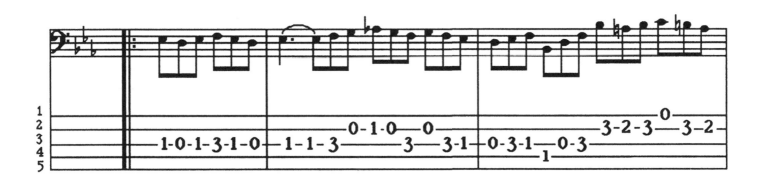